Good-bye Summer, Hello Fall

Written by Irma Singer
Illustrated by Bob Barner

Good-bye summer. Hello fall.

When summer ends, we say good-bye to summer fun.

But when fall comes, we have fun, too.
We go back to school.
We see our friends.

When fall comes, every day gets shorter.
Every night gets longer.

We say good-bye to peaches.
It's time to eat apples!

The green leaves turn red and yellow and brown. Then they start to fall.

More and more leaves fall off the trees.
Is that why we call this time fall?

When fall comes, the wind comes, too.

Birds fly by in the wind.
A warmer place is better for them now.

Fall is the best time to get pumpkins.
We spend our money on pumpkins.

Some pumpkins are round and fat.
Some pumpkins are tall.
We look for the best pumpkins!

There are more and more cold days.
The nights are colder, too.
We wear jackets when we rake the leaves.

We like to jump in the leaves.

Fall is the best time of all!